Our Little Black

Book of Ills

Our Little Black Book
of Ills

Expressions of Grief

Victoria Valentine   Lynda G. Bullerwell

jacob erin-cilberto   Amitabh Mitra

ISBN-13: 978-0692380956
ISBN-10: 0692380957

Published by Water Forest Press
PO Box 295, Stormville, NY 12582
WaterForestPress.com

Layout & Design by V.R. Valentine
Edited by P. Valentine

An extraordinary man ...

Tom

"Come to the edge."
"We can't. We're afraid."
"Come to the edge."
"We can't. We will fall!"
"Come to the edge."
And they came.
And he pushed them.
And they flew.

Guillaume Apollinaire,   1880-1918
French Poet, Philosopher

Victoria Valentine

Lynda G. Bullerwell

jacob erin-cilberto

Amitabh Mitra

Introduction
by Victoria Valentine

I've held so much emotion inside for over a year. Frozen. Blocked. Unable to find my voice, to complete the novel I started shortly before my husband fell seriously ill in February 2014. Something hit me the other night. The dam broke. And for several hours ... I wrote the poems you'll be reading in this book. The fact that I was able to once more do something so dear to my heart felt amazing, momentarily exhilarating, incredibly uplifting. Now that I've vented within the pages of this little book, which I call black because of the subject matter, existence feels somehow a bit more hopeful. What you're about to read is true. Is me. Is my life. I'm inviting you to share my inner thoughts: my husband's struggle. Mine.

Illness is rough on everyone involved. We're still trying to figure out who's hit the hardest: the person suffering physical pain ... or the caregivers on the emotional end facing an uncharted journey they never dreamed they'd have to endure. If you're looking for solemn poetry, and a peek into someone else's desperation, this book is for you. These words might make your life look better ... or worse. Either way, we hope you will take a chance on reading *Our Little Black Book of Ills*. Feedback is appreciated, as is spreading the word so that others can decide if our book is right for them. I have called upon three very dear friends ... three absolutely amazing poets ... to join me on this difficult voyage: Lynda G. Bullerwell, jacob erin-cilberto, Amitabh Mitra.
Thank you my dear friends and readers.

Victoria Valentine

My inspiration for this book is my husband, who was diagnosed with four thoracic sarcomas in February 2014. He underwent a surgery during which the surgeon left cancer inside his chest. At the time, he was given no alternative other than to wait for this lethal and rapidly spreading cancer to re-grow, which it did. Basically, the doctors wrote him off. They did not offer chemotherapy or radiation therapy. Their reasoning: his sarcoma would be drug resistant.

This devastating news prompted our tedious search for a second opinion thoracic specialist. We found an amazing surgeon in July, who offered a lifesaving technique which we were told could be curative. However, surgery had to wait until private healthcare kicked in, which would be several months later. The poem, *Falling into Shock*, represents our trip to Texas where my husband was scheduled for this extensive curative surgery in October 2014. However, when his chest was opened it was discovered we had waited too long: the cancer had broken through his chest wall and tentacles reached under his rib cage. It was inoperable. Anything after this point would not be curative: it would be life extension only. After waiting nerve wracking months for the surgery date to arrive, this disappointment seemed the final blow. Utter shock. Helplessness. Frustration. Anger at the system which had not permitted him private healthcare because we had applied after the enrollment period.

We returned to New York where my husband began a very strong regime of chemo, six infusions in total, one every three weeks. As I write this letter and format this book, he has received his fourth dose. The fact that the excruciating chest pain he had been experiencing is just about gone gives us hope that the cancer might be shrinking enough to return to Texas for that third and hopefully lifesaving surgery: if it's God's will, perhaps in February or March 2015. Three days from today, on Tuesday, 1/27/15, a PET scan will reveal the answer. This seems an endless waiting game, and waiting can near unbearable. Throughout this ordeal, the impatient me has learned patience: the control freak in me to relinquish. As always, my husband has remained strong but solemn. There is no such thing as hopeless if you try to have faith. Take one day at a time. Find peace in any way you can. Love one another as if there is no tomorrow.
Thank you and God Bless.

1) Update: We've been sidetracked yet again. This time by a monster blizzard which decided to strike on the exact day of the PET scan. The scan is rescheduled for Monday February 2, 2015.

2) Update: The imaging center had a cancellation on the day after the storm! So we didn't have to wait until Monday (tomorrow from today, as I write this) The PET was done on Wednesday, January 28, 2015. Hopefully, prayerfully, I picked the results up the next day. Sadly, his condition has deteriorated. Because his pain had been relieved, and some days he felt quite well, we were certain the cancer had responded to treatment and we'd be heading to Texas for another shot at surgery. Unfortunately, the chemo did not work. The cancer spread even deeper inside the right thorax and metastasized to his spine. :(I'm still in shock. After a year of disappointment, I was certain we'd be on the uptrend and 2016 would be a better year. After all that's transpired, how can I still experience disappointment? Another cliché: always expect the unexpected.

You're drawn, waxen / sleeping an entire day without waking
I tiptoe in every few heartbeats / to see if you're still breathing
I watch I wait / while cells divide / so not ready to say goodbye

Cancer (scourge not zodiac)

I'm fastidious
tend daily to laundry and chores
immaculate fingernails ... claw
walls / waiting / watching / wondering
my heart
hurts when I see his pain
pains when his eyes pass through me
with that one-dimensional stare
like a ghost refusing to depart
my heart
breaks
soars when he awakens
hopes when he smiles
gently / barely / laboring
like my thoughts, his words are fragile
still ...
my mind
struggles to reason / clings to fantasy
this year will certainly fare better than the last
will rally with health, rejoice with relief
it must! I find myself imploring
without bending a knee
yet nonstop I pray
surely instinct to survive fills my lungs
heart and mind relentlessly agree
this wretched life must one day render peace

Falling into Shock

I still taste the warm breath of Texas
although we are back in New York
where bitter snow burdens
branches of our pines
On the balcony we stood
gushing over fountains
marveling at thirsty palms
reaching for the cushion of sky
The storm swept in without warning
spinning our heads
like the earth that threatened to
hurl us off its back
out into space / separate us further
Your fight for life
plucked every flower
from your meadow
I stood with the futile breeze
as midnight devoured us

Hope

I think we should move to another galaxy
perhaps settle on a planet like Mars
where little green men are powerful
hold sterile wands in alien hands
and cure you with one wave
You would stand on a
glistening mountain peak
where your chest would expand
and your voice would fill the universe

Hopeless

I walk on the ledge of a skyscraper
windows are sealed
no door in sight
They claim memories are stored inside
I have this distressing case of amnesia
No wonder!
Now they say stress will cause this
But I think it's something dreadful
Ah ha ... now I realize
You are locked inside this building
and I am stuck perched near the roof
unable to pull you into my arms
I'm not suffering amnesia
I am helpless

Dancing with the stars

Another sleepless night of writing
my mind won't let me rest
Dreaming up romantic verse
to disguise your failing body
Days I carry trays
and dole out pills
What I hate most about writing
is my antagonistic brain
which
won't let my weary soul
close down for the night

I wouldn't have a bucket list
I already have a hit list
Of course I would not kill anyone
Just swear at the things I hate
like writing until my brain is raw

My head is like Gitmo
filled with insanity
like a prisoner calls out for freedom
my thoughts cry out for voice
now I wish for morning
when I will rise and see you again

later that day ...

You asked what I would do if you died
I'll meet you up in heaven, I replied
and we'll go dancing with the stars

Sounds

Your moans are mournful
or is it the wind
resting her limbs on the sash
sighing to alert me
reality will soon break down the door

Prolific

Why I hate writing
it's a curse
words cry for release and I won't let them
because sleep is important to care for you
still ... they bang at my skull until resentfully I snatch a pen
and in the dark of night, roll onto my side, clutching paper
my mattress is warm
you are in the other room ... cooling

Cake

I gaze through the window
sipping tea
watching robins
thanking God for the
breath of today
wondering what His plan is
for tomorrow / on edge / always on edge
when from the corner of my eye
I spot the Entenmann's box
shut it or you'll wake the kids
but they've grown in their own homes
while he was away
and I've used blonde to cover up gray
strangers I entrust with my innermost secrets
but will anyone know the truth of it all?
the difference between distressing and de-stressing
is vast
reaching in with a fork
I swipe a good mouthful
not tasting the sweetness

making way down my throat
then it's downstairs to jog
my usual two miles
then tend to the life I pray
survives more than one day
the mind never stops
though the limbs want to cave
while poems skirt the skull
that later will contemplate
let music fill the air
tonight belongs to me
no more stressing
I'm decompressing
for supper I'll eat cake
then tuck myself in
and dream with my pen

Cliches

In one palm my rosary
in the other Mom's keys
I sit and I wait for my heart to slow
while machines stir the air
probing / scanning
my grip tightens
along with my chest
Mom hasn't held these keys
for over twenty years
but I'm sure she's that angel
who is closer to Christ than me
waiting is the worst part or so they say
I can vouch for this however

time ... so much time / yet never enough
I've known him most of my life
now he's fighting for his
ours
stretched out on a table
at the mercy of men
time and time again
only time will tell
time is of the essence
time is on our side
time flows
so do years / tears

Kamikaze Pilot

My hand goes to my mouth
my heart to my throat
it's so heavy
I can barely swallow
maybe it's my thyroid
who the hell knows
but today he's the patient
and I must be strong
the doctor is compassionate
rendering a diagnosis
rarer than bloody roast beef for Christ's sake!
there's nothing we can do
other than pump you up with toxins
which may or may not work for
sarcoma / he calls it such a hideous word
we'll try anything / just tell us
tell us there is hope
have you ever seen a helpless doctor?
is this expression for real or rehearsed?
angry: me disbelief: you
what the hell? my mind screams
point zero zero one percent?
why couldn't you have hit lotto?
what are you doing to us? to me?
blame seems easier than acceptance

cancer is an ugly word
no one is ugly
you are beautiful
cancer is evil: the sound of it: the smell: the appearance
its restrictions
it backs you into a corner / throttles / blinds
binds your arms and legs
until you are insignificant
I'm here for you
to help heal your psyche / your body
until you are strong enough to stand again
on your own
care for me like you used to
in more ways than one
for many years I've been alone
disease has brought us closer
such a shame life cannot be reversed
I find I'm mourning
before you're even gone
take advantage of every moment they say
tell me how to do this
do I sit on his lap? crush his frailness?
or drag him onto mine ... but wait
I can't sit in one place longer than a moment or two
restless mind ... anxious bladder
put me on my feet so I can care for you
hold me up while I lift your morale
fight! I scream at the lover in me
it's all up to you
take this flight / crash if you have to / just fly

Bones

from your deathbed you command
as you've done standing
all these years
call me careless
I've imagined you dead
then faced your empty chair
and to date I remain devoted
taunted by uncontrollable thoughts
what would life be without you?
I shut down and reconsider
we'll make it through this
when I step through the threshold
of my private room
the presence is so strong
if you were not still with me
I would swear it was your spirit
determined to haunt me

if not you, then
it must be my mom's sensitive soul
here to offer comfort
or possibly to heal
some days when I miss you
I watch your sleeping face
pale / mouth slack / so fragile
and I wonder if you're dreaming
are you sad? are you frightened?
are you still with me?
the erratic rise and fall
of your skeletal chest
replies

While Waiting

let's eat chocolate
and watch a movie
there must be more today
than chemo-
therapy is what I need
but not through an IV bag
I need to toss my body
through the air
scream until I'm hoarse
while you watch and laugh
then I'll pull you from your chair
and brace your limbs with mine
dance you around the room
and sing into your ear

your disease has cost you thirty pounds
stress has claimed twenty-five of mine
which is a thrilling loss
feeling light of body is good for me
light of heart even better
can I have both?
hell ... can I have it all?
you, me, movies and candy?
we'll tip the scales
and champagne glasses
when Tuesday's test says: remission
but oh the waiting could drive me insane
what do we do if our dream is just
another nightmare?

Loving You without saying

chemo
vomiting
chemo
toilets
chemo
medication
chemo
trays
chemo
mood swings (us)
chemo
fears (mine)
chemo
cranky (you)
chemo
here's my shoulder ...
I'm right here

Numbly
(for Marian)

Leaning over you,
numbly I kissed the side of your cooling face
They say dead people look like they are sleeping:
You did not look asleep
You appeared as if your soul had just taken flight
Yet we all knew it had years before
(wanting ... waiting to be with dad)

Peering through the window
I watched the sun surrender to a tumultuous sky
For ten minutes, a miniature tornado furiously assaulted
the street's grit, heaving thunderous sentinels of rain

Maybe that is when you truly took flight

When I left the building my legs weakened
and I crumbled onto the cleansed wet sidewalk
Amidst a flood of memories and droplets of misty sky
I found my way home, alone

Was that sudden burst of brilliance in the clouds
You slipping through heaven's door?

I would like to think so...

Fly With Me
(in the dead of night)

In silence she came unto my bedside
Sleepy were my thoughts
Churning and jumbled
Yet aware
That I could reach out and touch her
Still, Her presence I denied
No I will not hear you!

With fervor she persisted
As did my lack of acceptance

Burst forth a dam of recognition
And resignation
Released from within my loitering depths;
Her advantage
Within moments
Her power unleashed
In the beat of one's heart in panic
And confusion

Mine!

With fury she came about me
Mastering my mind
Wrapping my soul with hers
Fear not she conveyed

Limbs shuddering
As an object bound for flight
Yet body grounded in vibration
Chest heaving with her thunder,
Gasping in disbelief
Turbulence engulfed me
As she tried to take me

Fly with me!
Her intentions forced stark
Reality

I shall show you far beyond
Your earth, your moon, your stars,
Places of wonder
Where I have journeyed
Let me take you there

No storm dare mime her violence
I felt her burning desire to lead me
Lift me not! I cried without sound
For I fear my life will end
Should I follow your path
And furious strength of will

(continued)

Although I fought for focus
And balance of the spirit which
Was no longer mine
I fast became the smallest particle
In a void of time
Insignificant breathless creature
Helpless as her essence drained
My struggling lungs of trembling air

Fly with me! Again her demand
But I could not
Perhaps I did not want to
Perhaps I feared
But truly I believed
In a heart that had been broken
With loss

For most precious as she had been
To me in life
Had I followed her that night
Surely mine would have ended

As hers had months before

And as sudden as her arrival
Was her departure.
She must have understood
I could not taste for a moment
The glory of her new world, for
In that same beat of a heart in panic
She set me free

About Victoria Valentine

I write poetry and children's storybooks as Victoria Valentine, steamy romance, horror and thrillers as January Valentine. My desire to be part of a rock band brought me into a recording studio, where my lyrics sprang to life with the help of a local alternative rock band. Together, we produced a music CD.

I enjoy designing books and indie publishing. In my free time, I hike and swim. I love all kinds of music. Watching horror flicks and Tyler Perry movies are my escape from reality. I'm an SOA and Walking Dead freak who would love to be a real life vampire.

I have an addiction to engraved pens, flashlights, tote bags, and a variety of cool stuff I buy to accompany each of my books. My office is filled with paperbacks and swag dedicated to my five novels which can be found on my Amazon author page and on my websites: Wheel Wolf, Fighting For You, Beautiful Experiment, Sweet Dreams in the Mind of a Serial Killer, Love Dreams. I have three novels in the works. Some day I hope to complete them. Years ago, I released a romance poetry collection: Desert Noon as Victoria Valentine

http://www.januaryvalentine.com
Victoriavalentine.net   LostPoetry.com
http://www.amazon.com/January-Valentine/e/B007Q28DFE
http://www.amazon.com/Victoria-Valentine/e/B005LYVSTM
http://victoriaskyline.blogspot.com/
http://januaryvalentine.blogspot.com/
https://www.youtube.com/WaterForestPress

Lynda G. Bullerwell

I try to be the one who thinks positive, believes in miracles and that everything will be alright. I tell everyone else that, appear strong, but late at night, when I have prayed myself to tears, I am scared like everyone else. This book is about fear, grief, and how I attempt to cope with illnesses of those that I love and the death of my best friend, which, on March 30 of this year, will be 20 years. As I type this, it is still so difficult to believe. I am thankful for my faith, my loved ones to comfort me, and the ability to be able to write it out which is often the only way to ease the pain. I hope that my expression of emotion may help someone, even if just to let them know that another person can identify with their pain. Thank you for reading!

If Solace Had an Address

One foot in quicksand
and another ready to run

to laughter, to love;

to anywhere that brings light
to ivory cheeks
too long hidden from the sun.

If solace had an address,
I would have sent myself long ago;
grew wings and left fear
in the murky waters

of a fragile life
so far in the distance

that is doesn't even echo anymore.

Blues

Stars fell

like the twinkle
leaving my eyes
and moonlight froze on still water;

my heart beating to every lonely chord.

When walls are thin

and skin grows thick to weather the storm
of syllables' piercing blows,

feathers bloom into wings.

Lips form whispers
melting every hue of blues

away.

Lament of a Caged Bird

Had they left the door open,
pulled the cover off
to shine the sun,

you may have sung more sweetly;
danced with wings unfurled.

If you could have breathed
this sea breeze,
watched ships sail in the distance,

you may have flown

or fared well in gardens,
branches
or even in your tiny cage,

but they nailed down the window-
no access to a ledge,

even in spring

when flocks join in chorus
with other winged beauty
and petaled mirth.

I see you dark now
with paleness;
no breath of tomorrows,
only winter

and you never liked the cold.

Sonnets Stitched in Blues

When whites are gray
and petals wither
like whispers, unheard,
rivers spill secrets in torrents;
every drop, a hymn
echoed through misty mountains
upon deaf ears.

Can fireflies save the night
when stars refuse to shine?

We can see the sun
through an abstract lens,
paint a pretty picture
before all the green is gone
and find synonyms for beauty
stitched in sonnets to leave behind
before senses are too dull to imagine.

Resuscitation

Whispers speak softly
to cheeks when tears
tell another story.

Love is the remedy
for pain; the flower
bringing scent of glory
to gray colored days

kissing night winds
with sweet chords
of pure silence

when no words are needed
to breathe life

into a once shadowed place.

Cover Me

I hear music
when we lie here, quiet;
see stars peeking through curtains
as two silhouettes dance

to the sweet sound of silence
with only breaths
and my heart

skipping beats, softly
afraid to awaken you,

but, somehow, you always know.

You turn to whisper me to sighs
of anticipation

and cover me

in a blanket as warm as your smile;
fingertips tracing my expression
and gradually gracing all but my thoughts

trading tears for giggles

when emotions are spent

on all the love
that I can handle.

Halo

There are soft echoes
beyond life's giggles
where we dare to dance
into the pitter patter of harp strings
within heart's intricate contours.

If you can bear the ache;

the loss of Spring
to the chill of Winter,

bare feet shall feel flowers
of purest petal
as love finds a resting place;

sun's radiant glow
riding upon your halo.

Saving Grace

Before adversity digs in its heals
on my winding pathway to fate,

wishing for blissful sleep,
I come to you on bended knees
begging for comfort; for clarity of mind

and your light never fails to shine

lending warmth to hollow places,
solace to cloudy shades of uncertainty;
tranquility to once shattered spirit.

Now, my rivers run quiet; ripples of hope
spilling into what were once only dreams
of something as simple and complicated

as love.

Little White Roses

There are things I could hate
like white roses,
falling stars

and anything chocolate,

but that would not bring
you back
or make my heart whole

again.

Too many springs
have come and gone quietly
without you on the porch swing;

laughter filling silent air.

All of these little coincidences
that keep you here
in spirit

are like the gifts you gave
just because.

It does not get better
like wine, with age
and I can't drink away memories

but rather get drunk on them
and pen pieces of us.

For Eloy

I dreamed you appeared before me
dressed in white,
air- brushed wings;
a glow about your presence.
There was a hymn softly playing
and a choir of backup singers

because that is how *you*
would make an entrance.

I knew that first night, when the star fell
that you would never be far from me;

light brushes across my hair,
breezes tickling my cheeks
when winds were still,

a sky filled with fireflies

and an unplanted cactus
blooming yellow flowers,
overnight.

I miss your laugh, your loving eyes
and the white roses you sent
just because.

I miss **you**,

but, deep down, I know you are here
watching over me like you always have.

There is a tree that stands tall
with branches that cannot be broken
by winds, rains, human hands

or even death.

Whispers of Fate

There are splinters that stick,
blades that shatter,
and waves of discontent

attempting to drown the soul,

but, there is a will;
whispers of faith,
never failing

and clarity

through clouds of dismay;
the path to passion,
a daunting expedition.

Call it an adventure;
a wistful pirouette
into arms of acceptance.

Kiss of fate joins hands
with silent participants;
stars that linger
watching love from a distance;

half-moon glances enticing waters
to wave me home.

Song of the Lark

Song of the lark echoes
where feet once tread
among fields of red;
poppies, watered with tears
of mothers, fathers;
bouquets carried by lovers

and generations
that would never be.

The flowers, they wait
for sunrise to spread love
glimmering upon once beaming faces;
ambitious ambiance kissing wounds.

The poppies, they salute
rising tall, only to rest
when sun sets

upon new born dreams.

When Letters Begin to Fade

I wish I could find the syllables
to express sorrow;

these phrases
fluttering from my chest
like a thousand fireflies
fighting for some space to glow
for you.

As we turn more silver,
wise, whispered, loving things,
devotion is the only thing gold

that remembers to stay.

I will bring you
every crystal constellation
wrapped in ribbons
of moon-laced shimmer
and if ever you forget this melting;
this affection that lingers
long after letters begin to fade,

take this sweetest lullaby with you.
to sleep,
so that nothing but dreams

separate

two symmetric hearts.

Gentle Path

Never say goodnight

to stars that whisper lullabies;
my head upon your chest
after darkness of the day.

Keep your fingers
intertwined with mine
as we stumble
over stepping stones
with jagged edges

like hearts, torn
before love
brought threads of Spring.

I can follow any winding road,

if you keep steering
dancing a gentle path
whatever the weather.

Sway of Willow

We never got to sway
together on that porch swing
or feel the breeze

that only country roads can stir.

Butterflies still dance
in my memories and I see you
in fireflies;
hear your voice feeding me syllables
to spill in poetry like this.

You are the passion
behind my smile;
the courage
that helped me hold your hand

when you took your last breath.

Someday, I will have that porch swing;
with each glimmer of summer
and shimmer of constellations upon my face,
I will feel you beside me

like the sway
of a weeping willow.

About Lynda G. Bullerwell

Lynda G. Bullerwell resides in Texas with her husband, Tim and her Autistic son, Junior. She is also the proud Mother of two daughters, and 3 beautiful grandchildren. Lynda has been writing poetry for over 30 years and considers it her passion and a release for emotions since she was a child. Lynda released a collection of poetry entitled "Into the Light" published on October 16, 2013 by Water Forest Press, and has been published in literary magazines including Hudson View, Skyline Review, Epiphany Magazine, Writefromwrong, Miracle e-zine and Struggle magazine.

Amazon Author Page: http://www.amazon.com/Crackers-Poetry-Collection-Lynda-Bullerwell-ebook/dp/B00SQAUYI4

jacob erin-cilberto

Life is short, and sometimes we find it feels even shorter as we lose loved ones through failed health or failed relationships. We need to hold onto the good moments hard and fast, make the most of them while they last.

There was a Time

what did you see?
when your eyes still saw happenstance
among circumstance
but reason left you,
when nothing made sense anymore
except the sense that nothing was there

except weeks, or days
of sand emptying from the hour glass mind

the tilting of history
so many years written into a life
a backlog of dreams waiting to prosper
fantasies committed to fruition
but the tuition invalid
the checks never balanced enough
to warrant coming true,
not all of them,

but already enough had played out
and you danced within them

closed your eyes and believed in what there was
what there could be
what you saw in him,

and you lived with that sense of engagement—
passion,
day to day exhilaration even for the simplest of things
even the mundane having meaning,

and then you closed your eyes one more time
dreams drifted just out of reach
sense, their companion,

and love,
it just kept sleeping.

More than a Flicker

your radiant blonde seared
with artificial rays
dancing in a house of mirrored flame
you were always the spirited mare never tamed

but always running toward the moon
figuring no dream was too distant to lasso
as your fingers strummed a tune
and your soft voice struggled to match steps

with a fiery soul that gamboled within you and without
those orange demons flitted about
like rude guests taking over your abode
then leaving with not so much as a "goodbye/thank you" note

they just embered out
a misguided thief
as you collapsed us in grief

and even the moon cried.

A Chance of Regrets

scattered showers
produce scattered flowers

a profusion of tears
allays the confusion and fears

as love tries to bloom
but ephemeral buds turn tribulations

all too soon.

Overwhelmed

waves of turmoil
in rain dance deciphering
a steady drizzle
confusion in reasoning

the calm feels
so far away
as the two barely touch
but it's enough.

notes of illusion

comatose blues
jazzy internship of clouded stigma

who are we really
but trumpets and horns of desired debauchery

foot stomping through life
with notes of triumph blazing through a cafe
of nostalgic defiance

playing a tune of traverse
with minds lost in the smoky haze
of make-believe martyrdom

sitting at overturned tables
chairs bound to the floor of misguided intention

thinking God is Louie Armstrong
singing "What a Wonderful World"

with a cracked voice
and a tear in his eye

Directions to a Lost Heart

meet me on the corner of
Flummoxed and Bewildered

i will love you till
your complexion turns to perplexion

your inquisitive skin
to befuddlement

and you wander through your wonder
with a MapQuest of detoured solution

to find me standing in disillusion
paving my way to you through dreams

that always seem one street over
from where i am

and you not able to understand
why you can't wake me.

Feeling an Old Draft

Camelot
contrary signatures
rental cars
rental coffins
roses smeared with blood
pink skirt to match
exploding interests
a back seat to rumbling
hair trigger effects
thumbs down
a courtesy call to heaven
here comes the bride accelerating
with white gloved tears

he lost his breath that day
exhaled through a head wound
and we lost a knight

in armor, that was penetrable
and had less of a shine
than imagined,
but then fairy tales
are never quite what they seem
are they?

The Taxi and the Ghost

i wander empty New York streets
in my mind,
wondering where the traffic of my inspiration
has driven off to

i am a maddening cab
with no fare
and it's not fair
that the back seat of my memory
should have no passenger

i am both driver and shotgun semantics
running some kind of insolent meter
that wants me to pay up with tears
but won't let me steer away my fears
and repression of foot
as i too carefully inch down the blockage of my thoughts
avoiding the speed limit reality
using my cruise control fantasies

to keep me coasting with a half smile
because if i accelerate
the other half of that expression
will scare me into bountiful impression

that runs over pedestrians
without so much as tempered deliberation
because a road without you in it
is a yellow line for me to cross
with reckless abandon

so i can just crash the idea of us
into scattered images
of crushed metal
have my heart rebuilt
with a new engine
the body of my self-esteem
restored

and write my way out of the city
of sad, permanently
with the windows down
and scent of starting over

staring at me
like a statue of St. Christopher
on the dashboard of forever
with the odometer in reverse.

Tomorrows Lost in Yesterdays

i can't stop walking those city blocks
my inner vision treading miles of concrete logic
but the few grass spots of vulnerability
are growing on my old imagination

maybe "a tree does grow in brooklyn"
but maybe a mind grows weary of skyscraper theory
we reach stories high in acceleration of thoughts
we write several floors of reflection
the windows of those buildings
mirror the lives we scrawl on the walls

graffiti memory
painted pristine
like a chapel of blues
the one sanctuary
from what we don't want to open
the vault of voluptuous vacancy

that which makes our feet blister
the mirage of lawns never encountered
there is no softness to the structure
of what has been built brick by brick

of evolution
and we, in our Darwinian diameter

are half souls
searching the radius to the circle
of a life that is the treeless jungle
of eventuality we just can't imagine
our way out of...

Outburst

teardrops fall from a gray sky
i feel you in each one
tapping the roof of my memory
pitter patter reminders
of the day you were,

24 hours of life, capsulized,
changing hues daily
escaping into blue
you taught me words,
that gamboled even under clouds
of whimsy
of adolescent query

i learned,
i wrote
i felt the tempest diminish
saw you dissipate
like a melting rainbow—

and even though your color
has left my sky
even in the midst of a pouring reflection

you dance in my mind
and i am still learning words
of you.

Synthetic Rhapsody

the blues image
of a mirror mannequin
lifeless parts,
heartless fingers
heavy window dressing
typing plastic poems
as others pass by and stare
wondering if they could wear that mantra

the poet with no soul
just a conveyance of supposition
in predisposed words
that reflect the neon lights
of the real life
on the undulating streets that
this mannequin will never walk again

metaphors are figurative parlays
into literal meanings we never secure again
once we lose the incentive

to face ourselves
and write what matters.

A Tear's Vision

love lazed
in a recliner
declining
the lining

of my poetic plea
sit with me—
please
sit with me—

so we might be inclined
to realign
to the design
of the stars peeking through

the curtain
so certain
you could assuage my hurtin'
heart

if only your sky
would comply
and make the blue depart
from the break in my eye.

Cold Sun

not much warmth in the ground
as the urn touches earth
a heart laid to rest,
watching from a tree branch above
suddenly, life is separation
the limb grazes a morose shoulder

a tapping sound
as the words touch a sunset
you were that one cloud
that determinedly clasped an orange sky

and we blinked the tears
as the emptiness started to fill
the holes in our horizon.

a Vermont Waltz

she's a pretty figurine
dancing in a bulb
of snow lit memory

an older version of a 1950's
Pendleton jacket
spinning within the fall leaves
crystalline passage
herself
a golden leaf,

still warm
as the frost
tucks her in...

Unkind Dust

creation, cruel joke
the rib splintered composes the mate
like a song that has imperfect grooves
towards the end
the label says pain

the bones become brittle
the record of life warped
until it can no longer play

the tunes spinning in my head now
remind me of certain lyrics you taught me over time

i memorized them,
and now alone,
sing them in the shower
as i futilely attempt,
to wash away the pain

but the soothing soap of sustainability
is just not strong enough
to do so.

About jacob erin-cilberto

jacob erin-cilberto, originally from Bronx, NY, now resides in Carbondale, Illinois. erin-cilberto has been writing and publishing poetry since 1970. He currently teaches at John A. Logan and Shawnee Community colleges in Southern Illinois.

His work has appeared in numerous small magazines and journals including: Café Review, Skyline Magazine, Hudson View, Wind Journal, Pegasus, Parnassus and others. erin-cilberto also writes reviews of poetry books for Chiron Review, Skyline Review, Birchbrook Press and others. He has reviewed books by B.Z Niditch, Michael Miller, Barry Wallenstein, Marcus Rome, musician Tom Maclear and others. Intersection Blues his lucky 13th book of poetry is available through Water Forest Press, Stormville, NY. His previous two books an Abstract Waltz and Used Lanterns are also available through Water Forest Press. His books are also available on Barnes and Noble.com and Amazon.com as well as Goodreads. erin-cilberto has been nominated for a Pushcart Prize in Poetry in 2006-2007-2008 and again in 2010. He teaches poetry workshops for Heartland Writers Guild, Southern Illinois Writers Guild and Union County Writers Guild.

Amazon Author Page: http://www.amazon.com/Jacob-Erin-Cilberto/e/B004APEVAG

Amitabh Mitra

We live in galaxies, immortality is just a space. In our physical minutiae, alien visitations of viruses and vagrants seem to demean our shared living. In such galaxies we live with the living. Behind closed eyes and a closed darkness, there resides the life. The virus is a life too. Its living seems unending; its mind a succession of evolution patterns, there is no dying for it in assumptions and denials. The human and the virus in an intangible enforcement seek a place in darkness or dawn. The mind as much as it reveals the virus, cortical neurones and synapses can unclasp it. Believing is far more important even if it means believing the sky or the earth or just a bird in the sky. Only then the mind takes you then on a roller coaster drive, peace consumes us. The virus an unearthly creature thrives in physical tantrums, Thinking and running in different strata unclasps this living within the living. Have you ever leapt out falling vertically downwards, have your thoughts raced in time seeking people you have left behind. The virus lives in this inability, inability to seek, it needs the earth and earth forms to navigate. If only pandemics can be defined in abstraction of a flower in a dew drop, if each human resolve to evolve too, if we can shed the narrow revelations, the virus an illiterate droplet gets crushed never to pass on. The CD4 Cell Count and the Viral Load are expressions of unforgiving nature of defeat and distress. It's another life proliferating.... The virus cannot thrive in such unreasonable destinies. Humans living in structures give shelter to it. In living we can prolong our mind to galaxies and far beyond, the virus can never reach. In death it cannot take the impenetrable, yet in living in stretches of combat, violence in perfect peace is possible. In an orange noon death throes of the unbelieving living within continues, diminished within a glass compartment getting tinier, its end reflects in forceful thoughts. Day dawns by itself.

The flower
In a dewdrop
On a sunshine
Over a single
Leaf
Rolling
To
Fall
At a corner
Life holds
It in
A balancing act
The flower
In a dew drop......

(Published in Adam Donaldson Powell's poetry book, Jisei: Death Poems)

16 Poems

1

Trauma lurks behind close doors and open streets in Mdantsane. It was the same before 1994 and even after that. You may ask me, what's so important about trauma, isn't it everywhere in the world. But this here is so different. People instead have lost feeling pain. Trauma occurs in slices of repeated contours as a sun bleeds every day. People don't remember having seen a slaughtered season so many times. Yesterday in the deepest dark I encountered a young girl. She was perspiring in fits, her mind jumped in crystalline splinters of cocaine. I could see her only through a sieve of old scars. She tells me in a distance her heart feels like a Sahel drought when blood trickles and disappears, her tongue swollen with many memories and the sand. She was a migratory bird, her conviction now lost to the many suns she dared dreaming again. Somewhere in a developed country, you browse through books and people. Academia is a reason and building smoother roads, juggling with history and future is trying hypothesis in refrained units. In Mdantsane, we just don't conclude. Back home when it rained you had once said, it feels as if the sky wants to share its river with us. What could we have shared with the sky then?

2

In an intense composite when ragged lacerations hobble in, its late night or even early hours of the morning, babbling to implant their cut off noses or ears. They had brought them, wrapped in a cloth like a man wearing only half a dress or the sun coming close, very close to dying. Somebody had tried enclosing the head in a plastic bag. Even Van Gogh's cut ear could not be repaired. I remember while doing post mortems, the skill was in cleverly hiding the suture lines. Yet in a world so intensely divided, sometimes we even shrink to the tiniest atom, thoughts benignly wake up daily to its usual toast and tea remembering always to close the door. Forgetting is never a habitual closure; tiny papules always leave a mark. The earth stretched even to space, just a place again to re-shelf infinite memories, each of them joined to the other in many lives we live simultaneously. South Africa rejoiced in its emergent democracy in 1994, at the same time 30,000 Tutsis were slaughtered and maimed on a single day at Rwanda.

3

And I always think of you and our lives at Old Delhi where we crossed many such borders and many such suns, just to know, we are still there. I remember you once refused to talk to me in the night of a thousand halos; it was the night of the *Eid.* Living that night with you is the fibril joining me to tomorrow. Vincent's last words were, this sadness will last forever. I live rejoicing such sadness, believing in a belief within my many crowded moments, you will always be there.

4

in transkei
we drove on roads beyond roads
the sun and the sky set themselves apart
and people there talked about new south africa
I wanted to get braids done on the
roadside
and dance to hip-hop
with others
being played by a blind musician
his head moving
his eyes behind dark glasses
negating all
nothing has really changed
only the dog among hitchhikers
just wanted to cross the street.

5

febrile convulsions
the road to mdantsane
jumps of arrhythmia
twists in contortion
of an impending stroke
nobody here watches
streets dying
the shacks rasping
sells us still
unconfined freedom
layers of elements and
longings
a river of so many people
touched the sun
the sky
with their
fist
once.

6

a strange river snaked within mdantsane
shaking the sky of remembrances
black rain tinged with blood made cesspools
hunger is an imagination
smirking at doors and lost streets
tapping at windows long closed
I had thought of you and the river
and our parting forsaking another innocence
an orange moulds the mdantsane sky
thoughts of yet another day

7

the somali spaza shop at street corner
mdantsane
beckons
the needy
cramped within
it too waits for
a stray bullet
or a
stab
violence is Islamic
in distant african shores
death
has no color
here
in peaceful
mdantsane
only the muezzins strange strain
sets a few birds
to flight.

8

and the one legged man dreamt at
cecilia
his prosthesis may perhaps be repaired
he probably wont get pressure sores anymore
some socks ...
come winter
he remembers a phantom leg
and the excruciating pain
more than that day
shot by
apla* members
he still doesn't understand
why they didn't kill him
why they shot him, a black pastor
why they laughed at the end
why is liberation so precious now
APLA was the Armed Wing of the Pan African Congress

9

earthy constrictions
and a wheeze
a river stopped
and a sky topples
unabated.

10

a child smiles
laughter runs amid narrow streets
takes a turn
and runs amok with grey
sodden clouds
and then it rains in mdantsane
heavy downpour
weeping
all its miseries in one go
leaking into shacks and homes
a drenched sun waits
clouds take their own time
to go home

11

mdantsane trains go to east london
and comes back
between streets shacks and a solitary sky
people go to work
people come back home
their loneliness blossoms
within the train
amidst daily familiarity
there is nothing beyond
each other's eyes
there is nothing
when we reach home

12

lulama hurries home
mdantsane enters a war zone
an evening creeping into a shelter
of spoken shadows
a dying night screams somewhere
the last breath snatched without pity
happiness now brims in the slaughter
of the unforgotten

13

there is no sleep
and these bloody sleeping tablets
brings back always the pain
addiction is pain
blackening the moon
blackening the dreams
black is where i live and i ask
you in wakefulness
why straying is combat
in an approaching desert storm
and lives just happen during that time
of birds, dogs and trees
restless
as another culprit night
demises in ardent failure

i deny another day
think of you
and throttle my car
towards a land
unheard off

14

ma ngobo lives in the far stretches
of scenery park
a tiny house amidst shacks and shanties
seems to challenge still
an unburnt sky
lush greenery in abundance
has taken over the tiredness
of old thoughts
flaming tyres around necks
and a flaming jungle
are as remote
as long lost anc promises
i often drink here to
the laughter of myths
a rebellion of conscience
seems so far.

15

daytime drags its feet
reeling under a broken sun
mdantsane moves
on its streets and paths
shacks and houses
sharing secret truce with
an emaciated river sky
last night tumbled
onto a today
 not quite understanding its reason
of another existence

16

it has been nights
i have spoken to walls
the floor on a soft thud
tries remembering history
skies correlate to different suns
nights always remain the same
patient
from many takeovers
people here seem
faceless
healing stays
structural as always
tonight
lets just talk again
of fears
in the eyes of man
he wakes only tomorrow
his shack
suffocating
under a strange new sun in
mdantsane

About Amitabh Mitra

Amitabh Mitra is an artist, poet and a medical doctor based in East London, South Africa. He heads the Department of Emergency Medicine at a tertiary hospital in Mdantsane. Mdantsane is the second biggest black township after Soweto. Most of these poems are relating to his daily involvement with trauma and assault at the hospital there and were published with his drawings as a coffee table book titled *Mdantsane Breathing* in *2010*. He believes in fusing healing with multiculturalism, realising socioeconomic gaps are the disease itself.

Website: http://www.amitabhmitra.com